A Selfie with my great grandparents

Kenzo Benjamin

PAIVEPO SERIES 1.2

First published 2017

© Kenzo Benjamin

Text: Kenzo Benjamin

Illustrations © Kudzai Mervin Chikurunhe and Seth Juelz Ndaba

The right of Kenzo Benjamin, Kudzai Chikurunhe and Seth Juelz Ndaba to be identified as author and illustrators respectively of this work has been asserted by them in accordance with the Copyright, Designs and Patents Act 1988.

No part of this book may be reproduced, transmitted or stored in an information retrieval system or by any means graphic, electronic or mechanical, including photocopying, taping or recording without prior written permission from the publisher. All rights reserved.

ISBN 978-0-9931361-3-9

Ignish Publishing House. UK

Table of Contents

Chapter 1. Preparing to go on holiday 3

    CHAPTER 2   The flight 6

        CHAPTER 3   Great granddad's home in the city of Harare 8

            CHAPTER 4   Visiting places of interest 12

                CHAPTER 5   Great granddad's home in the village 16

                    CHAPTER 6   The Selfie 26

Chapter 1. Preparing to go on holiday

My name is Kenzo. I am eleven years old. My mother, Lisa, is British and my dad, Tino is Zimbabwean. I live with my sister Bethel, mum and dad in London, England. All my grandparents live in London close to my home. After the end of my Primary School Leaving Examinations, my nan (grandmother or ambuya), Lorna, from my dad's family, offered to take me on holiday to Zimbabwe for four weeks of the school break.

This was not my first visit with my great grandparents, Synos and Gladys, at their homes in Harare and in Murehwa. I had been to Zimbabwe many times, mostly with my dad when he was on leave from work. I had also spent a whole year in Harare, the capital city, with nan Lorna when I was 8 years old. I had stayed at nan's house in Borrowdale Brookes and attended a private school in Borrowdale. I made many friends I was still in contact with. I learned a lot of things about the country and improved my basic speaking and writing skills in the two main local languages in Zimbabwe, Shona and Ndebele. I learned to play guitar and drums during that year. My dad wanted me to get to know that side of my heritage. Dad always said that a wise person had said, 'A people who do not know their history will not know where they are going and will repeat the same mistakes made by ancestors.'

Nan Lorna set three conditions for going with me on holiday to Zimbabwe; that I would pack a whole suitcase of new children's clothes, shoes of different sizes and toys to give those in need; that I would be willing to learn from anyone and that I should never take without giving. I agreed to meet the conditions although I was not sure I would fulfil them.

Nan was very much into humanitarian work. Her holidays were never just about sightseeing and being on the beach. Don't get me wrong, nan had fun during her holidays. She believed that each person can make a difference in others' lives. Nan made it a point to help other people either financially or by spending time making a difference in their lives. She volunteered to teach or spend a day helping in a care home for children, old people or the disabled. She always said that whatever one is good at is meant to help other people and make life better. Her favourite saying is, 'There is more joy in giving than receiving.' Even in London, she volunteered at an old age home once a week, worked four days a week and she spend Saturdays with her grandchildren.

My parents packed my suitcases. My mum packed another suitcase with all clothes that I could no longer fit into. She made sure that they were not torn. She also asked me to pack the toys that my sister and I had outgrown. We closed school in July. I had to wait ten days for my nan who had to complete some project she had been working on. I was so excited about my holiday that during that waiting period, I made sure I caught up with all my friends in Zimbabwe on social media. It was summer holiday for me in the UK, but it was the middle of winter in Zimbabwe with temperatures around 18 degrees, which to me was warm. Mum and dad took me to the doctor. I got my vaccination against Malaria before my flight. My mother made sure I had a lot of hats, slippers and sneakers and some warm clothes. Mum did not worry about me being away from home. She knew that I was very independent and that I liked to learn by exploration.

In my family, my dad supports one football team, my mum a different team, the two grandfathers are fans of different teams. Any football game we watch at home is always interesting because of these different teams. The good thing is that each of them wanted me to support their team. They had all bought me T-shirts and shorts for their teams. When dad's or mum's team was playing, I wore the full kit to watch the match with mum and dad. However, when dad and mum's teams played against each other, I went to visit the grandparents because I did not want to take sides. My football T-shirts were now a little too tight for me. I packed all these in my suitcases.

I asked my parents to buy football T-shirts for my grandparents as presents. They each bought one from their own team. Great grandfather's shirt was imprinted with his name and the number 5 for the day he was born. Great grandmother's T-shirt had her name and the number 11. My two nans were not football fans. They bought me a football and a guitar to take with me on holiday. They also added a lot of different story books for children and some games including a chess board. My two grandfathers bought many T-shirts and shorts for boys and girls. I watched as my sister, Bethel, lovingly placed her dolls and their clothes in a mini baby chair in my suitcase. She said I should give them to little girls who don't have dolls. Bethel loved those dolls and I knew she was giving them with love. I made a mental note to video the donation of those dolls so that Bethel would know the dolls were going to be cherished.

Chapter 2.   The flight

The flight was long, 11 hours. I slept through most of the flight. Nan Lorna read for a while from one of the many books she always keeps and then fell asleep. I woke up at intervals to go to the bathroom. I remember looking out of the window and seeing a brown, dry area on the ground which seemed to go on for miles, for hours and hours. It was the Sahara Desert. I peered into the darkness another time I awoke and saw that we were still flying over the desert. The next time I woke up it was early Thursday morning. The Air hostess woke me up. The view of the ground through the window had changed. There was a lot of greenery.

I went to the bathroom, washed my face and brushed my teeth. I got my hand luggage out to look at the time on my iPad. Just then there was an announcement, 'This is your captain speaking, we will be landing in Harare in 15 minutes. We hope you had a pleasant flight. Thank you for flying with us!' We had a smooth landing. We walked to the Customs and Immigration building. I could see people on the balcony of the airport building, waving to us as we walked away from the plane. We went through Customs and Immigration with no problems although there were long queues. I surprised one of the officers by greeting him in vernacular. I was glad that he did not go on speaking in Shona as he would have exposed my limited vocabulary.

The great grandparents met us at Harare International airport. Their driver, Gilbert, was a family friend who was flying to Bulawayo, one of the main cities. It was great to see them. They commented on how tall I had grown. Great granddad said that he had been watching from the airport balcony and had seen us walk from the plane. Gilbert helped us to load our many suitcases into great granddad's car. Great grand dad took me upstairs on the elevator at the airport to watch planes landing and taking off. This was exciting. We watched Gilbert and other passengers walk to their plane. Twenty minutes later an Air Zimbabwe plane took off for Bulawayo with Gilbert in it.

I was fascinated watching different planes from many parts of the world landing and taking off. We had breakfast at the airport restaurant on the balcony. The plane we had arrived in taxied on the airport runway and then took off headed for South Africa. After breakfast, nan Lorna drove great granddad's SUV from the airport. We drove to their home in the suburbs of Harare passing by open woodland areas as the airport is built out of the city. There was a lot of traffic in the city centre. It was busy in the city. The sun was shining and there were people standing against walls basking in the sun.

Outside the city's main park, nan Lorna stopped the car and parked. She turned to me and said that I could go and see my friend if I wanted. My friend is the ancient tortoise in the park. He lived in the corner of the park and was chewing on lettuce. He had grown bigger than the last time I was in the country. I took photographs of him. There were many children watching him eat his lettuce We passed many different residential areas to get home.

Chapter 3. Great granddad's home in the city of Harare

We arrived home from the airport just after midday. Great nan Gladys was 92 years old. She used to be a teacher in a primary school. Great grandfather Synos was 96 years old. He used to manage a clothing factory. They both walked very slowly but were still very alert in the mind. They had a home in the suburb of Vainona in Harare and a farm in rural Murehwa.

They welcomed me in their 4 bedroomed bungalow where they lived near Uncle Kudzai, nan Lorna's brother. I gave them the presents I had brought for them, long winter coats, and the sports T-shirts, a track suit for great grandfather and a winter dress for great grand nan. Following tradition, nan Lorna had advised me to buy a blanket for each of the great grandparents. They loved the presents. Great grandfather went to his bedroom and put on his sports shirt and track suit bottom. He came back to the lounge pretending to be a sports commentator and football player at the same time.

'Synos has the ball! Gladys tries to dribble it away! Synos kicks it to Kenzo! Kenzo uses his famous left foot and it's a goooooal!' We all laughed, and I took photos of him with his camera. Great nan teased him and challenged him to go and play real football. He just laughed and thanked me again for the presents.

I gave Uncle Davey, dad's brother, a T shirt with a picture of his favourite Formula 1 driver who has won many races. He lifted me up and put me down, saying, 'You are a great nephew, thank you.' Later, he drove out to the nearby shopping mall to get internet network connection for nan Lorna and a Sim card for local network for my phone.

The neighbours came to visit and soon children of my age followed. I knew some of these children from when I had spent a whole year in the country. I went outside with the children and made firm friends with Tafara and George who were our immediate neighbours. It was sunny but cold for most people. Many children played outside in the yard and we joined them. It was as if I have always played with them. There was always something fun to do. Although we had a ball, it was fun to make our own ball with plastics, to draw a makeshift football ground and play until we were exhausted. We drove toy, wire cars on long dirt roads. We played video games at one of the girls' home. George had a swimming pool at home, but everyone felt it was too cold to swim so we left that for another day. We had much fun playing 5 aside football on the makeshift football ground.

The next day was Friday. Nan Lorna had arranged for me to attend the last school day before the local school holidays at my friend George's government school. The school was within walking distance from home. I was one of the most popular students at school that day. The other popular students were Ruko, Thandie and Tanaka who were Zimbabweans on school holiday from USA, Japan and Germany.

The teachers gathered all primary school finishing students in the hall. We sat in three huge circles with the teachers. We discussed education in the different countries, music, technology, sports and fashion. I have never laughed so much. We were like a mini, fun, United nations gathering. There were a lot of different accents. Some students laughed at my accent and tried to imitate it, which caused even more laughter. There were just as many facilities' in the school as in my own school in London. There was not much schoolwork on that day, but we learned a lot from local and international students about many different places. I was asked many questions about my country. I made many friends. I did not know it until later that the school had arranged a musical event in the hall for the afternoon for all students from 3pm in the afternoon. I saw dance moves that were incredible. We all danced up to 5 pm when parents arrived to pick their children from school. George, Tafara and I walked with uncle Davey back home.

The next day, uncle Davey took Tafara, George and I to climb a hill after which Harare city is named. From its summit, you can see the city in all directions. Uncle Davey explained that Harare was named after this high point (Haarare means he does not sleep), where in the past the Shona chief had guards on this hilltop to look out for enemies. The climb was fun but hard. We saw some flame lilies on the way to the top. The flame lily is the national flower. Afterwards we went to an open barbecue place near a stadium. There was meat galore and we ate hungrily. There were many people eating and music was playing loudly. By the time I slept at great granddad's house that night, I was exhausted.

Nan Lorna took us to the museums, Water world and the Cinema in the city. She always parked at the city park for me to visit the ancient tortoise. On Sundays, we went to church with the great grandparents and we had lunch in a different restaurant every week. My great grandparents told me many stories about what my dad and his brothers Remi, Davey and Prince were like and what they did when they were young. Uncle Davey told us about his life in New Zealand. His wife and children were there. His business had a small branch in Harare so he was here for another three weeks on business. His children and I always kept in touch. I had been to his home but was too young to remember it. My dad had promised I would spend next year's summer holidays in New Zealand.

At the end of every day, I Skyped on nan Lorna's computer with my mum, dad, or my uncles, nan and granddad on mum's side of the family in London. Sometimes the great grandparents joined in the conversations. After the skype session, Great grandfather said,

'Modern people have faster ways of communicating across great distances. In my day, we wrote letters and would wait a month to get a reply!' Wow, I thought, that really was the old, ancient days and that they had a lot of patience.

Chapter 4.   Visiting places of interest

Nan Lorna, great grandparents and I visited Mosi-o-a-tunya, the smoke that thunders, (Victoria Falls), Manna pools, Hwange Game reserve, Chinhoyi caves, Great Zimbabwe and the hot springs in Mutare. We flew to and from these places of interest. I took many photographs and many video clips of the wildlife. Great Zimbabwe was a fascinating place. I tried to imagine how they had built the structures. At Mosi-o-a-tunya, the water thundered down, creating a spray. I bought post cards from each place we visited. We met many friendly people. Some asked me about their favourite English players. There were others who thought that I live near the famous players.

Uncle Davey and I spent half a day with Harare soapstone carvers and those who make wares from wire, clay, reeds and metal in Harare. These were skills passed down from father to son with no formal training involved. It was a great learning and humbling experience for me. The men and women were very patient with me. I made a tiny basket using reeds, a toy car with wire and a Zimbabwe bird with the soapstone. I was proud of the clay cups I made for Bethel, my mum and dad. I watched them being fire dried. The truth is that I got a lot of help to make all these things. I wanted to take home original presents for my family.

Working with metal looked a bit more complex. Uncle Davey said he did not want me to risk injury, so I just watched from a safe spot. He did not allow me to make anything from the liquid glass which was being blown into fantastic shapes. I thought all the people there were very talented. As they worked, they talked and made jokes. I bought presents for my dad, mum and grandparents from there. Afterwards, in the evening, uncle Davey took me to his office. He did some work for an hour. I was on the computer chatting with my mum and dad on Facebook. We went back home at 6:30 just in time for the evening meal.

Every day I slept immediately my head touched the pillow because I was so tired from different activities. Early in the morning, I would wash up, feed great grandfather's two Rhodesian Ridgeback dogs, water the flowers and vegetables for great grand nan, then I was free to do things with my friends. I had named these two dogs, Spike and Swift when I was 8 years old. Great grandfather had brought them as puppies when I had spent the year in the country. I remember spending great times with the puppies. You would find them all day gently following great grandfather or great nan. The minute someone rings the bell at the gate, the dogs seemed to change into their combat gear and start their equivalent of karate moves for dogs. They would leap and rush to the gate, barking menacingly at whoever was at the gate. Most of the time great grandfather kept them in their doghouse during the day. They patrolled the yard during the night. Great grandfather had made sure that the gate and wall around the house were high because the dogs had been known to jump over a lower gate. They were lovely dogs, but I am sure thieves thought twice before attempting anything.

After breakfast, some friends and I watched cartoons or a movie before going out to play. One of the best days of the holidays was when nan Lorna, my friends, George and Tafara and myself went to an orphanage in the city. We took along the suitcases of new and old clothes, toys and games I had brought from London. George and Tafara's mother also donated some of the boys' clothes. My sister's dolls were received with a lot of joy. My friends and I distributed the clothes and shoes to the children at the orphanage. Nan Lorna had brought even more clothes so that each of the 50 children in the orphanage got something. I chose 4 three-year-old girls to give

Bethels' dolls. Tafara made a video for me. The little girls' faces lit up with wide lovely smiles. I knew Bethel would be happy to see this. The girls shared their dolls and sat down to dress them.

At first the children thought that I talked funny, but they got used to my accent. I found that the language of play, fun, laughter, music, dance, invention of toys and curiosity, however, speaks louder than accent and it creates loving acceptance. We played many games including football. I gave my football T-shirts to children of my age. The children in the orphanage loved the football and guitar. We formed two football teams and played in their football ground. Later, their awesome Marimba club played music for us to express their appreciation for all we had done that day. A small girl called Chiedza played the African piano, Mbira, with a lot of passion. In my mind I thought on my next holiday I want to learn to play Marimba and mbira. We had lunch and supper with the children in the care home.

Unknown to me, nan Lorna had requested donations from uncle Davey's and other local companies for food and money. Nan Lorna had also brought along ten homeless people who were helping for the week at the Orphanage and she had paid them. The money was also used to pay some of the orphanage bills and to stock their pantry.

Some of orphans shared their life stories with us. Most of the stories were very painful. I found that hugs or hand holding were sometimes more comforting than words and that listening to the children helped them deal with pain. They were all attending school at a nearby government school. We discussed school and a few of them showed us their art and science projects. We left at 8 pm when most of them were going to bed. Before we left, the head boy and head girl made speeches giving thanks for the donations and for the time we had spent at the centre. The boarding mistress, whom they all called 'Gogo vaTapiwa', (Tapiwa's grandmother) said a prayer and all the children loudly said, 'Amen!' at the end. I felt humbled. I had met complete strangers who had made deep impact on me. I realised what having parents means. Tafara, George and I felt that this had been a great learning experience for us all and that we should not take our parents for granted. I phoned my parents before going to sleep. My parents were very happy that I had given away my clothes and toys selflessly. I told them that I wished I had had more to give.

Great granddad Synos told me that he was proud of me for giving to charity and spending time with the less privileged. To me, this was one of the best days of the holidays. I learned more on that day about value of family and the things we take for granted about parents. I learned from these orphaned children that they make the most of what is there and do their best in all things. They showed appreciation for the care they had at the centre. The appreciated the fact that we spend time with them. They shared what they had and developed their talents and skills. They had amazing resilience despite their painful life stories. I think nan Lorna wanted me to learn that I am privileged to have my parents, to learn to share with others, to learn that everyone has something to teach us and to learn about my culture.

Chapter 5.   Great granddad's home in the village

Before the final week of holidays, Nan Lorna drove me and the great grandparents to the village home in Murehwa. We drove for about two hours on a main road passing many farms on the way. We turned right onto a dust road and in 10 minutes we arrived at a huge yard with four large round huts and 2 rectangular huts. It was after 3 p.m. There were two solar panels and a windmill on the roof of the large rectangular hut. The smaller rectangular hut had a satellite dish. There was a gate and a hedge around the homestead. The car was parked inside the yard and we alighted and walked into the big round hut which is great nan's kitchen.

Two aunties, Ruth and Catherine, my dad's sisters, greeted us and welcomed me to the home.   Inside was a cushioned bench around part of the inside wall. There were two windows on either side of the door. There was a covered fireplace in the centre. A chimney rose from the fireplace to the centre of the grass roof. On one end of the bench was a large clay pot with a lid and calabash on top. The clay pot stores water and the calabash is used to get water to drink. There was also a wooden cabinet, a small sink, some utensils hanging from the wall and a small refrigerator. In the wall, there was a triangular indent with two light bulbs on the wall and electric switches. We sat down on the bench and great grandfather said, "Kenzo, this is your home. Welcome and feel free to go anywhere and to ask questions if you want to know anything. You have been here before and you know your way around."

Great grandfather said he was going to check on his cattle. I went with him to the other side of the huge yard where the cattle pen was enclosed with wooden planks and partly roofed. The cattle herders were just bringing the cattle back from pasture.

Great grandfather said he had 60 cattle and 6 calves, 10 goats and 18 sheep. The cattle, goats and sheep were enclosed in different pens, each with a big water container and a roofed area. Dung from the pens had been removed and left to dry in a pile. Great nan used it and the chicken manure as fertiliser in her vegetable garden.

I looked at the cattle horns, the huffs and held great grandfather's hand tightly. Some of the cattle and sheep looked at me as they were chewing grass as if they were saying to themselves, 'Who is this one? He looks scared of us!' Great grandfather must have read my thoughts. He laughed and said, 'Ahhh, Kenzo, you are afraid of the cattle? Your dad and his brothers were also scared when they were younger than you, hah hah hah!' He laughed loudly, throwing his head back.

Great grandfather held my hand and went on to tell me that when my dad, Tino, was young, my dad Tino, his brothers Bongani, Davey and Prince, and sisters Catherine and Ruth had visited with nan Lorna and their late father, Ronnie. They stayed for a week at the village. Tino, Prince, Bongani and Davey told great grandfather that they were tired of eating vegetarian meals in the village and wanted some meat. Great grandfather had taken his axe and gone with them to his cattle pen. He asked them to show him which cow they wanted him to slaughter for meat. The three boys ran back to their mother screaming and asking why great grandfather did not buy the meat from the supermarket like other people do. They were squeamish about slaughtering the cow. Although I laughed at the picture in my mind of my dad running from a cow, I was afraid of the big cows I was looking at. Their horns were enormous. Just then one of them went, 'Mooooo!' I almost ran away. I was sure that the ground shook. I remembered my U.K. nursery rhyme soft 'moo' sound. Oh, man, this sound was loud, forceful, vibrating, bold and unapologetic. I liked it although I was fearful. Great grand father held my hand and he started telling me the names of the cows. He touched some of them trying to reassure me that they are not scary.

We walked back home. Great grandfather pointed at the large 3 bedroomed hut near the gate. He told me that one was for his son, uncle Kudzai and his wife. They worked in the city. The second 3 bedroomed round hut was Uncle Davey's. Aunties Catherine and Ruth shared the 4 bedroomed round hut. They had their own houses in Harare. They both worked as nurses at the nearby hospital. The small round hut on wooden stilts was a storehouse for the harvest and seeds.

The roofed, mud walled rectangular hut was for meetings, barbecues and celebrations. It had toilets and shower at the back for public use. It was an interesting, large room with reed folding curtains which could be folded to let light into the room, animal skins on the floor and hand-crafted stools. On its roof there were solar panels and in the middle of the roof top there was a small windmill to provide energy in winter. No one slept in this room. It was the powerhouse for all the homes in the yard and for the lights in the cattle pen. Great grandfather said that uncle Kudzai and nan Lorna had modernised the homestead, putting solar power, running water, bathrooms, satellite dish and the small windmill. He said they had network for internet because their satellite dish connected them to the network at the nearby hospital. All the homestead toilets were connected, as were most of the villagers, to a biogas plant at the hospital. He said that his homestead was used as an example of sustainable development in a local textbook. He showed me the book later. Great granddad explained that traditionally, one built a round hut as the kitchen and a square hut as the bedroom. There was space, great granddad said, for my dad and uncles Prince and Bongani to build their own houses in the homestead.

The smaller shaded open area next to the kitchen was like a utility area for washing dishes and laundry. There were 4 large drums full of water here. One drum collected all water which fell on the roofs. One drum was connected to all the bathrooms another was connected to the kitchens and the last on was for the utility area.

There was a chicken run with more than 20 free range chickens and 8 baby chicks looking yellow and soft. We collected 18 eggs for breakfast. The 6 ducks were quaking away as if they owned the place. Outside great grandfather's yard there was a dust road and beyond that were all his fields. Behind the cattle pens, about 15 minutes' walk, was great grand nan's garden.

When we got back to the kitchen, food was ready. We all ate in the kitchen. Great grandfather sat on his self-sculptured mobile stool. I sat on the bench next to him. Soon after supper, a lot of relatives from the neighbourhood arrived and great grandfather proudly introduced me. The room was full. We went to the lounge in the small rectangular hut. Some stayed behind in the hut, talking, laughing, shelling groundnuts, some knitting. Great nan was grinding peanut butter. She was doing that on a smooth stone and with a small stone. Her movements were fast.

In the lounge, the television was switched on and we watched a local drama and the news as we ate popcorn. Beyond the lounge were two bedrooms and a bathroom. One was the great grandparents' bedroom and the other was where I was going to sleep. Although great grandfather reminded me about my bedtime, he let me stay listening to the stories some of the men were telling about the past.

I woke up the following morning in one of the bedrooms, I did not know how I got there. I went to the bathroom, washed up and walked to the kitchen, where I met great grandfather by the door. He was carrying a pitcher of milk, coming from the cattle pen.

He said, 'Good morning, Kenzo. If you are to run this farm in future, you have to get up early in the morning.' I promised I would try but that whole week I never woke up early. I had breakfast. Suddenly there were many children of my age who came to visit me. I knew most of them from my past visits. We fed and watered the chickens and ducks. We opened their coop to let them out.

Then we followed the cattle herders for a while. I saw huge anthills and the boys explained to me how that ants build these. We walked over a small stream by stepping on the rocks in the river. I watched the cows, goats and sheep eating grass. I came close enough to a cow to touch its face briefly. We climbed to the top of the Chiwere hill and had a magnificent view of the village. We talked about a lot of things. Other children asked questions about my home and I also learned about their daily routines. When we were hungry, we ran back home. Two of the boys, Tendai and Tawa, went to my great grandparents' home with me and we all sat down to eat a late lunch. Great nan did not mind me bringing them along and it is cultural to share food with everyone present.

After lunch, nan Lorna advised me to stay around the house as she wanted me to see great nan's garden and later to Skype my parents. She was pounding maize to make mealie meal. I was amazed that at her age, she never sat idle. I tried pounding but it was too hard for me. Great grandfather showed me how it is done but I knew it would take me a long time to learn. Great nan was sitting under a tree painting several of the clay pots she makes.

Later, I accompanied great nan Gladys and aunties Catherine and Ruth to great nan's garden. It was a big garden with a hedge and a gate. There were many beds of different vegetables and many fruit trees. In the centre was a borehole which was built up. There was a lever you pulled several times to bring the water up and then you turned the tap on. Buckets and clay pots are used to bring the water for drinking to the house. Every few days, they fill up two huge water drums from the borehole and used two yoked cows to pull the drums to the house so that they could have water for general household use. Great nan said the garden used to be nan Lorna's favourite exploration area when she was young.

Great nan insisted that I carry a tin of water, saying, 'A wise person said that until you carry your own water for some distance, you will waste water and not appreciate its value.'

Ruth, Catherine and great nun made twisted rings with pieces of cloth and placed them on their heads. Then they lifted their clay pots onto the ring. They walked tall and well balanced carrying a basket of either fruit or vegetables with one hand leaving the other hanging down freely. Wow! I knew that was a balancing act I would love to learn. I carried the tin full of water in my arms. I had tried carrying it on my head and failed. We walked back in a line along the footpath. I stopped many times to watch great nan, but she had no balancing problems and she never touched the clay pot on her head. I used the camera I had brought along in my pocket to take photos and video clips of these well poised women balancing clay pots so effortlessly. I saw a huge bull frog in a little swamp. I put my tin down and followed it as it leap-frogged off. I sat down to watch some ants which were carrying leaves and moving in a line. I poked a dung beetle which was rolling its hoard, but it concentrated on its task. Then I picked up the tin to keep up with great nan. I stopped again to watch a chameleon which was changing colour and a lizard which went up and down a tree. As I watched, great nan shouted, 'Kenzo, please keep up with us.' She had not even turned to look at what I was doing.

I asked her how she knew that I was doing other things. She laughed and said I was as curious as my dad and my nan used to be. By the time we arrived home, I had half the water in the tin because I kept spilling water as I stopped to take short video clips of anthills and long millipedes. Great grandmother looked at the water tin, laughed and tousled my hair. She said that nan Lorna used to break a lot of clay pots carrying water because of curiosity and exploration. She said I had the same level of curiosity and love of learning. Later I Skyped with mum and dad on great grandfather's laptop. My friends Tendai and Tawa also spoke to my parents. We had supper and this time I slept almost straight afterwards.

The rest of the weekdays were spent with Tendai and Tawa, who were also on school holidays. We explored the whole village and the surrounding grazing land and fields. I visited their homesteads and had a few lunches there. We went herding the goats, sheep and cattle with older boys and soon I was not scared of the animals. Everyone did some work in the field during the day. I did a bit of work, but great grandfather allowed me to go with my friends so that I learn more things from people of my own age.

We visited the local shopping centre where there was loud local music playing. Occasionally, some people would break into a dance to the music. These were regular people who were going about their own business who would just stop, put down whatever they were carrying and without a choreographer, they would dance in synchronicity. When they were tired, they would pick up their luggage and move on.

Everyone had a rhythm. I joined in the dance as it was free for all. We stayed at shopping centre for a while because of the music.

I enjoyed the evenings at great grandfather's home. The evenings were like attending a type of school with a varied syllabus. The teachers of this syllabi had expertise acquired from the university of 'oral information passed down from generation to generation.' In the evenings, the great grandparents' home always had visitors from the extended families who lived nearby. They brought along whatever project they were working on to pursue their talents. There were poets, embroiders, knitters, comedians, drum and mbira players, singers, dancers and those who made musical instruments. All these people did not have formal training, they learned by skills being passed down to them. In all these sessions we laughed so much my sides hurt. We gathered in the kitchen, the lounge or the celebrations hut. I often moved between the huts to get the best of both worlds. I was particularly interested in storytelling.

Stories were either about the past, about giants who lived in the past with giant feet like the footprint at 'Dombo ra Mwari' (rock with footstep of God) that nan and I saw in Epworth outside Harare. There were also stories about our national history or stories which had a lesson for the young people to learn. Everyone used their hands to do something whilst watching television or telling stories. Even the elderly people keep busy all day. People were crocheting, sewing, knitting, painting clay pots, making calabash cups, sculpturing, making wares from reeds or scrap materials and carvings which were sold in the nearest town at the month end. Uncle Timoti was carving out of soapstone. When I first met him, I could not make head or tail of what he was making until the sculpture of a man and woman with a baby on her back became clearer.

I went to the field with great grandfather for two half days. It was ploughing season. Villagers help each other to make work faster. I suppose this is the origin of the crowd funding concept. That week villagers were at my grandparents' home. There was a lot of food being cooked for their lunch. Great grandfather said the villagers would be back in a few weeks when the first rains fall to sow the seeds. As they worked, they sang and told jokes. Everyone understands and speaks English, so I did not have any problems, in fact, my conversational Shona improved. Nan had used most of the week to visit different relatives and sometimes she had gone with the great grandparents during the day.

I went on the local bus to the nearby hospital for great grandfather's medical check-up. The bus trip to and from the hospital was an experience I would like to repeat. The bus was full inside and it has a huge load on its roof. People joked, bantered and laughed about almost everything. The bus driver, who has known my great grandfather for a long time, called him, 'Master Farmer.' I liked this side of Great grandfather, light-hearted, making jokes and laughing. He introduced me with pride to the bus drivers as, 'This is the next Master Farmer, my great grandson, Kenzo!' Although the bus was full, they found a seat for me and my great grandfather. At the hospital, great grandfather had his check-up. We rode another bus back home after some shopping.

The day before we left the village, great grandfather summoned me to the celebrations hut in the yard. When I got there, there were many uncles, related to great grandfather, seating on stools in a circle. I had met all of them. I greeted them and sat on a stool next to great grandfather. He handed me a stool he had been carving and said that was a present from him for my dad. I was impressed by the craftsmanship and I thanked him on dad's behalf. He said that he had called us all to the meeting so that the uncles would witness and know that he was giving me my own cattle, two calves, a male and female. He said I could do what I want but he hoped that they would grow to be a large herd of cattle. He had given all other great grandchildren their own cattle. He reminded the uncles that the field near the river belongs to my dad. Great granddad turned to me and said, 'Kenzo, I have told you before that we, as a people, build wealth in cattle as well as money and other property. I guess this means you will have to come back and visit me more often to ensure that your cattle are well looked after?'

I did not expect such a great, living gift and was not sure what to say. I was very moved emotionally. I accepted the cattle, thanked him and said that my dad will know what to do. I said I would love to come back and visit him. I thanked all the uncles and asked them to look after the calves for me. As we walked to the cattle pen to see the calves, I thought that my friends back in London would laugh at me about my calves because they would not understand the culture. We took pictures of great granddad, me and the calves using my phone. This present made me feel very honoured.

Chapter 6.   The Selfie

I went home with great grandfather to find great nan sitting on a bench outside the kitchen. Great grandfather sat down next to her. She was on their Facebook page on nan Lorna's laptop. She had a magnifying glass to her face and one hand scrolling down the page. She showed great grandfather something on the page. There was something about their slow deliberate movements and clicks on the laptop, the village and hut setting and use of technology that I thought was worth remembering. I asked them if I could take a photo of both and they agreed, only if I was in the photo with them. They laughed and started narrating things from the past. I took selfies with my great grandparents.

Nan Lorna arrived just then. I asked her to upload several photos onto great nan's Facebook page; the selfie with the great grandparents, the photo with great grandfather, me and the two calves, and photos of great nan, nan and myself at Great Zimbabwe at Mosi-o-a-tunya.

The look on my great grand parents' faces when the photos were uploaded on Facebook was priceless. Almost immediately after being uploaded, there were many 'comments and likes' on the Facebook page and relatives were asking who the boy was. The selfie was not even a good one as I had later taken better ones. Great grand nan Gladys typed slowly with one hand, the other holding the magnifying glass to her eyes, 'This is our great grandson, Kenzo; the first born of the first born of our first born, Lorna. We are blessed to see the fourth generation.' Many more comments popped up and my grandparents stayed on Facebook for more than an hour lost in their own world.

The proud look on their faces made me realise that this was a great moment in family history. They talked about how that photo puts them in the records on Facebook for future generations to see them.

Great nan said that in their generation, they had few photos of their ancestors but that this selfie was linking them to the future. I decided, at that moment that, when I went home to London, I would take selfies with my great nan on my mother's side and for my family tree. I felt that I had made Synos and Gladys very proud and somehow linked the past to the present and catapulted them all to the future. I knew I would cherish these photos. To me, this was the highlight of the holiday. I had given the great grandparents something that was very meaningful to them at their age. They asked nan Lorna to upload all photos of all their great grandchildren onto the Facebook page. They said this would make it easy for us to make our family tree. Great nan said great granddad and herself would write notes on their family tree so that we would all know about our lineage which they knew orally.

Nan Lorna turned to me and said, 'Kenzo, you are a remarkable young man and I am proud of you. You have made two elderly people very happy.' I realised that, just by being myself, helping and doing what I could to the best of my ability, teaching others what I know and learning from them, that I had met the conditions nan Lorna had set for taking me on holiday in Zimbabwe. I had given things as well as my time. I had learned from many people and shared the knowledge I had. Although I saw some poor, disadvantaged people and places, this was not the norm. There are beautiful houses in the country in many places. People live in houses in their villages, towns and cities. They visit the game reserve to see wild animals. I had I travelled to many parts of the country, sometimes by road sometimes by air. I am proud of this side of my heritage as well as I am about the English side of me.

We left the village the following day after saying many goodbyes. Great Nan gave me a decorated clay cup with my name in embossed letters. There was also a cup with Bethel's name embossed. This brought tears to my eyes. I thanked great Nan and knew she had lovingly made the cups for us. I wrapped them in a towel. We left the grand parents in the village and we drove to Harare with Auntie Catherine who was going to stay at the great grand parents' home in town for a while.

In Harare, we went to the art shops to buy presents for my great nun, grandparents and my parents in London. Nan Lorna printed one of the selfies, framed it and left it in the great grandparent's bedroom in Vainona. I bought my mum a metallic flame lily, the national flower. Nan Lorna sent the presents by DHL because they were heavy. I said many more goodbyes in Harare to the many friends I had made.

Nan Lorna and I flew back to London. I slept for most of that flight. My parents were waiting for me at the airport. I had had an awesome holiday, had a deep tan to prove it but realised that I had really missed my mum and dad. I started secondary school within a few days of coming back from holiday.

Sadly, 8 months later, great grandfather Synos died peacefully in his sleep. Nan Lorna, my mum, dad, my sister Bethel and I flew back to Zimbabwe to attend the funeral. Great nan Gladys was distraught. All dad's siblings and their children flew in for the funeral. For once all great grandchildren were in Zimbabwe at the same time. All his eight great grandchildren treated the funeral as a celebration of life for the man who had taught us so many things, whose laughter we could still hear in our minds. This man had made us proud of who we are through imparting practical knowledge and wisdom.

Great grandfather Synos used to say, 'I have a duty to empty what I know into you, my great grandchildren because when you know what

I know, you discover new knowledge and add onto what I teach you. You should then be able to pass on a lot more knowledge to your children.' We knew about our Zimbabwean heritage because of him. He had a way of explaining history so that he took us, his audience, with him into all the events he described even though some were from way back in his youth. Great grandfather Synos was a great man. He once surprised us by saying that he learns from us especially in terms of technology. We reminisced on the history of technology that he told us and how they used to think that a telegram was sending information fast when it used to take days. He used to advise us to share knowledge humbly. Six of the eight great grandchildren were living outside Zimbabwe. We all knew how to do things many local people had forgotten. Although our parents had given birth to us, great granddad Synos had planted us in the local soil. We designed the funeral programme and put many photos of the different stages of his life. Nan Lorna and her brother Kudzai oversaw the whole programme. Great nan was in shock and was trying to cope. People from her side of the family attended the funeral in large numbers. We all tried to comfort great nan as much as we could.

His funeral was held at the village. More than 200 people attended it. We sang some of the songs he had taught us. It started with a church service followed by many speeches. Great grandfather Synos was well known by many people. When he was being buried was when all 8 of us broke down to cry. I think the reality hit us then, the great grandchildren, at that point. I was sobbing uncontrollably, with great drops of tears running down my face. Parents comforted us. After the burial, we went back to the homestead. We felt empty. Catering was done by the daughters-in-law of the family. Food was served to all the people gathered. It was strange not to have great grandfather there. His clothes were distributed to his relatives. I was given his sculptured stool. Great grandfather had made a will, leaving his property to his wife, his daughter nan Lorna and his son Kudzai. The grandchildren, my father his siblings and cousins, inherited land and money. All the eight great grandchildren inherited money and cattle. After the funeral the eight grandchildren took many selfies with great nan which she posted on Facebook happily.

The funeral was also an opportunity to learn about culture. People get together with the bereaved family. Family grieve and moan and they are comforted by the extended family and the community. The daughters-in-law of the deceased's family are responsible for the catering. Sons-in-law are responsible for carrying the coffin and placing it in the grave. Elders make decisions in consultation with immediate family. Grand children and great grandchildren play the role of ensuring all systems work properly and carry out instructions according to wishes of the family. Aunties and uncles offer comfort to the immediate family and ensure that all procedures are carried out according to culture.

The community works together to ensure that the funeral goes well, so no one has a funeral alone. Much later, a year or two after the death, the gravestone is laid. There is always plenty of food at funerals. A joke is told of a homeless man who arrived at a funeral, crying loudly and looking distraught. People thought that he was a close relative and they made way for him and gave him water and food. He took out spices from his jacket pocket and spiced his food. Then, when he finished eating, he took out his toothpick to clean his teeth and he asked, 'Who died here?' The man was not related to anyone there, he just wanted a free meal.

Our family stayed in the village for a week keeping great nan company. We then flew back to London because of school and our parents' jobs. Nan Lorna stayed for 3 months looking after her mother.